Titles in the series:

The Fox	0241 11215 X
The Mouse	0241 11213 3
The Pigeon	0241 11214 1
The Squirrel	0241 11216 8

Design by Linda Rogers Associates

First Published in Great Britain 1984 by
Hamish Hamilton Children's Books
Garden House, 57–59 Long Acre, London WC2E 9JZ
Copyright © 1984 by Joyce Pope
Copyright © Illustrations 1984 by Elizabeth Goss
British Library Cataloguing in Publication Data
Pope, Joyce
The fox.—(Animals in towns)
1. Foxes—Juvenile literature
2. Cities and towns—Juvenile literature
I. Title   II. Series
599.74′442   QL737.C2
ISBN 0-241-11215-X

Typeset by Katerprint Co. Ltd, Oxford
Printed in Singapore by
Tien Wah Press (Pte.) Ltd.

Animals in Towns

The Fox

Joyce Pope

Illustrated by Elizabeth Goss

Hamish Hamilton · London

The fox was tired, so tired, but he dared not sleep. Throughout the long September day, he lay panting in the drainpipe on the building site. His nose twitched at the unfamiliar smells, and his ears pricked up at the sounds of men and machinery.

He was little more than a cub, and only yesterday he had been playing with his four brothers and sisters outside their den. But last night, instead of following his parents when they went hunting, he turned in the opposite direction. He ran alone across the fields until, lost, he reached an iron fence. He paused a moment, then slipped under it.

Suddenly, he found himself in a different world, with no grass or trees, but smooth grey pavements and road. As he stood, he heard a dreadful roaring, and saw a monster with eyes like two yellow moons snorting towards him. Without thinking, he ran. Seeing the fox in his headlights, the lorry driver smiled. 'Cheeky beggar,' he said to himself. 'I'll give him a run for his money.' And he slowed slightly to keep just behind the galloping cub.

After a couple of kilometres, the lorry turned off, and the fox slowed to a walk. He was in the middle of a town. The street lights frightened him, so he turned down a narrow alley. It led into a maze of little streets. He padded softly past rows of small, grimy houses, and eventually came to an open space. Here the old buildings had been knocked down and new ones were being put up. Wiry grasses and weeds had sprung up among the bricks and concrete.

4

The fox discovered a puddle and drank thirstily. But all he found to eat was a beetle, which he quickly crunched up. As the sky grew lighter above the chimney pots, he knew that he must hide. He squeezed into a drainpipe and stayed there the whole day.

When the builders had finally gone and the noise had stopped, the fox felt it was safe to leave his hiding place. He crept out and explored the building site. But finding nothing to eat, he set off again, keeping to the shadows of the small streets.

This time he was lucky. The roads led to the town park, and one of the trees gave him his first meal – a feast of crab apples which had fallen to the ground. Better still, he smelled meat. He tracked the scent to an old sausage roll and some sandwiches in a litter bin. At first, he dared not touch the metal, and he circled the bin for a long while. But, at last, hunger overcame caution and he jumped into the bin and gobbled up every last crumb.

The fox lived well in the park. He ate scraps of food left by the visitors, and when this was not enough, he clawed for earthworms in the flower-beds. Once or twice he caught a vole, pouncing on it and killing it with a quick shake, just as he had seen his parents do. He hid and slept during the daytime under the dropping branches of a thorny bush. Here he could lie dry and secure, even when the weather was bad.

People came and walked and played and shouted, often quite close to him, but they never knew he was there. He soon learned not to fear the noise or smell of humans, though he was always on the look-out for dogs. He was chased by them several times. But he had a number of hiding places, including one which he reached by scrabbling up the sloping trunk of an old tree, and so he always escaped.

7

As the year wore on, the park became a less good place to live. There were fewer people and food grew scarce. One freezing November night, when there was nothing at all to eat, he turned once more to the town.

The fox had already learned that the lights and some of the smells of the town did not mean danger. He took no notice of the acid smell of people, which hung everywhere among the buildings. And he ignored the stink of petrol and diesel fumes from cars and lorries. But he was always alert for signs of something new – they might mean danger or food.

He soon realised that the town was a far richer place to live than the park. Behind the town hall was a tiny overgrown garden, and in one corner stood a tumbledown shed. The fox made his winter home in a hole under the floorboards, and here he spent most of his days. Although he knew several other safe places, none was as warm or secret as this.

He found his food a little further out of town, in the dustbins outside houses and blocks of flats. He became very clever at nosing the lids off the bins so that he could explore inside.

Hungry foxes will eat almost anything and this one was no exception. Bread, bones, overripe fruit, all sorts of table scraps – nothing came amiss. One night, he found the almost complete remains of a chicken. It was too much for him to eat at once, so he carried it back to the garden behind the town hall. He buried it in a shallow hole, pushing the soil over it with his nose.

Usually, the restaurants in the main streets were very careful to tidy away waste food so that animals could not get at it. But one night the fox found a delicious-smelling bag in the gutter. Inside was a half-eaten hamburger and some chips, which somebody had dropped. The meat was gone in one gulp. The chips were not so tempting, but just as he was about to tackle them, he noticed something move in the shadows.

10

The fox paused, and a creature that he had never seen
before stepped towards him. It was a stray cat searching,
like him, for scraps of food. The cat's fur was standing on
end, and its tail was fluffed out like a bottle brush. The two
animals faced each other, then the cat took another step
forward. The fox, always wary of anything that he did not
know, turned and ran, leaving the food. But the cat did not
like the chips, and only licked the paper, so the fox returned
later and finished his unusual meal.

By late December the fox was full grown. His fine reddish-brown coat was thick and glossy, and his brush-like tail had a white tip. He felt that the town was his permanent home and though he saw no other foxes, everywhere he went he marked the ground and bushes with drops of strong-smelling urine. This was his way of claiming the area as his living space, and warning off other animals.

One night, as he travelled towards one of his best feeding places, he came upon a new smell. It was so interesting that it attracted him even more than the thought of food, and so he followed it. The scent led him across much of his territory, then towards the gardens of some suburban houses, which he was afraid to enter.

Two nights later, as he crossed the town square, he heard a strange sound. Three short, wailing cries – Yip-yip-yawoo – repeated again and again. The fox called back, a harsh, howling bark, and set out in the direction of the cries. The powerful scent filled his nostrils. Soon he tracked down their source – a beautiful young vixen, with a thick russet coat and white-tipped brush, just like his own.

As the fox approached, the vixen ran away. When he followed, she turned and snapped her sharp white teeth at him. He leapt back and kept his distance. But he did not give up, and the following two nights he went to where the young vixen lived.

Eventually, his patience was rewarded. Instead of snapping, she greeted him with her mouth open and her lips drawn back in a sort of smile. Briefly they touched noses and then carried on searching for food.

In the cold winter nights, they found a new place to look. Many people put bread and suet on bird tables for the hungry finches and titmice which lived in their gardens. Often the foxes finished what the birds had left, being agile enough to jump on to the tables. Sometimes, they caught a mouse which had slipped outdoors to look for food.

When they had fed, they played, chasing and dancing round each other, and sometimes standing on their hind legs, with their paws on each other's shoulders. They often sang their unmusical calls to each other, but the few people who heard them thought the weird noises were made by birds.

In February, the weather turned very cold and there was less food. One night, the vixen found a pigeon which had died, weakened by the winter weather. She swallowed it in one mouthful – feathers, feet, beak – the lot. Both foxes often dared the street lights to pass take-away food shops where people threw bits of spare ribs or chicken bones into the gutter.

One night it became so cold that the pond in the park froze over. The fox had often stood on the bank smelling the plump ducks which roosted on the island in the middle of the water. Now, suddenly, he could walk across to them.

The sleeping mallards had no idea he was coming until one drake was seized by the neck. The bird flapped and struggled, but it was soon over. The fox was not only bigger, but made desperate by hunger. All the other birds scattered, squawking loudly. But the fox was satisfied, and carried his prize to a safe place. Although it was too big to swallow whole, he ate all of it except for the tough wing feathers, which he sheared off with his sharp teeth.

The fox caught no more ducks, because the next day a thaw set in and the ice melted. In spite of this, the birds on the island slept fitfully for several nights.

In late February, the fox and the vixen mated. It made little difference to their way of life, for they still lived apart. And though they played and hunted together, each ate the food that he or she caught.

In early April, the vixen became restless, and she moved from her usual den to one near her mate's home. She dug out a new, deep hole under a shed on the edge of some disused allotments. Here, in the middle of the month, her four cubs were born.

The roly-poly babies looked very different from their parents. Their faces were short and blunt, their ears were folded down against their heads, and though they were covered with fur, it was short and grey. They huddled against their mother for warmth. She never left them, feeding them with her milk, and washing them with her long pink tongue.

The fox was doubly busy now, for he had to find food for his mate as well as for himself. Luckily there were mice on the old allotments; and early one morning he caught four baby ducklings which had lost their mother. Only when his mate was fed did the fox think of food for himself, and it was often light before he slipped back to the safety of his den.

When her family was three weeks old, the vixen moved from the nursery. The cubs' eyes were open, though they still couldn't see very well; and their fur, which was longer and fluffier, was now dark brown. At first, she often returned to check that all was well and to feed them milk.

By the time they were four weeks old, their teeth began to show through their gums and she brought them earthworms and mice as their first solid food. Their father worked harder than ever to find enough bones and scraps in the town.

As they grew, the cubs needed more and more food. When they were eight weeks old, their mother had no more milk for them and they had to rely on what the adults could catch and share with them.

One warm evening in late May the cubs left their nursery for the first time. The big world was full of strange shapes and smells and shadows. But for the time being, they played tag and king of the castle, with their parents looking on. As they grew bigger, their games grew rougher, though the old foxes stopped any fight before a cub was hurt.

As they played, the cubs learned many things – such as how
to leap on prey, and how to fight back if they were attacked.
Sometimes, their mother would bring back a live beetle, or
some other small animal, and they would pounce on it, and
shake and bite it, to make a kill, just as they would have to
do when they were grown up and on their own.

Sometimes, if he found a specially big piece of food, the fox
would take it to the nursery. When the cubs ran to greet
him, he would turn and trot slowly away, and the cubs
would follow, tumbling over each other to get at the meat.
The vixen would join in the game, and they all shared the
food. But mostly the adults brought food for their family,
and then guarded the young ones as they played.

When the cubs were three months old, they went beyond their playground by the old shed for the first time. They wanted to explore everything, but they stayed close to their parents. By following, they found out where to look for food, and how to catch it.

At last, in the autumn, the cubs began to hunt on their own. By now, they were nearly grown up and had to leave the family den. Perhaps they would go back to the country, or maybe they would find a place in the suburbs. But their parents were town foxes, and would live close to people in the shelter of buildings for the rest of their lives.

Everything in this book is true. Many foxes do live in towns, often right among houses and shops. They are very wary, so they are not easy to see. But in some places where they are certain that nobody will hurt them, they may come out during the day and sunbathe, often lying on the roof of a shed, or some other place where they can see and smell possible danger.

They learn not to be afraid of trains. If you are travelling by train, look out of the window and you might be lucky enough to see one on an embankment or shed roof.

Foxes are often very clever at discovering food in dustbins, finding ways to knock the lids off so that they can get at the titbits. If something knocks the lid off your dustbin at night, it could be a fox.

Foxes in towns sometimes kill birds in parks. Often they do not eat the big flight feathers, but cut them off, as you can see in the drawing.

Look for fox footprints in mud or snow. Foxes walk on their toes, like dogs do, but their footprints are oval, with small pads and lots of hair between the toes. Look at the drawing to see the difference between fox and dog footprints.

A fox may chew the ends
of feathers as it bites them off.

Fox
footprints.

A fox does not usually waste much food,
but may leave some bones and skin –
like these pieces of hedgehog.

Dog
footprints.

25